When the Beasts Spoke Blessing
Being an Orthodox Meditation on Saints and Animals

by
Sulien V. Solovyov

When the Beasts Spoke Blessing: Being an Orthodox Meditation on Saints and Animals by Sulien V. Solovyov ISBN: 9781989647844 First published October 17, 2025 Toronto, Ontario, Canada

Publisher: The Evergreen Centre

Publisher's Cataloging-in-Publication Data

Solovyov, Sulien V. When the Beasts Spoke Blessing: Being an Orthodox Meditation on Saints and Animals / Sulien V. Solovyov. – First edition.

Summary: This volume serves as an Orthodox Meditation on Saints and Animals and a Threshold to a Hagiographic Odyssey. It explores the true, shimmering lore of holy ones whose sight was so cleansed that they saw creatures not as mere beasts, but as kin, as fellow icons of the Living God. The book asserts that all creation is a theophany—a visible manifestation of God's invisible glory—and seeks to reclaim the primordial dialogue of benediction. The work is a call to discern the difference between authentic, Christ-centered compassion and a secular, utilitarian movement that sees the animal as a tool for deconstructing human exceptionalism. It includes accounts of temporary restorations of unfallen dialogue, such as St Kevin and the Blackbird, St Cuthbert and the Otters, St Brendan (and the whale Jasconius), St Hilda and the Swans, St Tryphon and the Falcons, and the manifestation of Archangel Michael through the Mountain Hawk. The narratives illustrate the theological principles of the Animal as Icon and the potential for Theosis in the Ktisis (Creation), demonstrating that creation, though groaning under the cosmic illness of the Fall, yearns toward redemption in Christ.

Identifiers: ISBN 9781989647844

Subjects: Orthodox Christianity | Saints | Hagiography | Animals–Religious Aspects | Theophany | Theosis | Creation Theology | Piety.

Classification: 270.2–dc23

When the Beasts Spoke Blessing
Being an Orthodox Meditation on Saints and Animals

by
Sulien V. Solovyov

Table of Contents

Foreword: When the Beasts Spoke Blessing
Introduction to a Poetic Journey

The storytellers of the old lands—of the high Slavic North, the deep German woods, and the mist-shrouded Irish isles— always told tales of magic and of the fearful wonder that dwells beyond the firelight.

They spoke of beasts transformed by dark sorcery and of ancient paths where curses held long sway.

But what if we, the hearers, had mistaken the whispers all along? What if the creatures, when they truly spoke, did not speak of the shadow, but of the blessing?

It is the nature of the wild world to offer a harsh face: the bitter cold, the hidden snare, the sudden flash of tooth and claw. But this book holds the true, shimmering lore: the accounts of holy ones whose hearts were so clear, whose sight was so cleansed, that they saw the creatures of the earth not as mere beasts, but as kin, as fellow icons of the Living God, veiled in fur, fin, and feather. This is the Threshold to a Hagiographic Odyssey, where the boundaries between the praying human soul and the vast, singing natural world vanished like morning mist.

The ancient Fathers and Mothers of the Church taught that all creation is a theophany—a visible manifestation of God's invisible glory. These tales serve as our windows into that truth. They are accounts of those few who understood the primordial dialogue, the original tongue spoken in Eden—a language of pure love, where every feather, every flash of fur, every resonant note was a prayer in itself. Here, in the lives of the Saints, the curse of separation is lifted, and we are reminded that the human and the wild share one single, ascending song.

We invite you to cross this threshold with reverence. Leave the noisy, crowded world behind and step into the silent glen, the open ocean, and the vast, vaulted sky, where the language of holiness is taught by the blackbird, the otter, and the whale. For in these simple, life-affirming miracles, we hear the deep truth: that creation yearns not for fear, but for communion, and that when the beasts spoke, they spoke only of the eternal, abiding grace of God.

Threshold to a Hagiographic Odyssey

O Lord Sabaoth, Sovereign of the noetic and sensible realms, Fount of existence and Bestower of every supernal boon: Thou hast enrobed the terrestrial orb in splendor and symphony, And suffused the empyrean with paeans from every quickened breath.

From the least of fledglings to the leviathan of the abyss, From verdant vale to unscaled peak, all Thy handiwork resounds: In feather, fin, and fur, Thy uncreated glory is proclaimed, A ceaseless theophany of Thy illimitable compassions.

Thou hast summoned Thy elect, who communed in theosis with wild kin, Holy ones discerning Thy icon in every limb and lineament. With contrite spirits, we cross this limen into their sacred lore, To hearken once more to the primordial dialogue of benediction.

Vouchsafe us, O Word Incarnate, the charism of this primordial chant, That we may decipher the lex of untamed solitudes, And immolate praise through every creature's transfigured strain— As all creation, deified in Thy light, ascends the ladder of divine union.

Glory to the Father, and to the Son, and to the Holy Spirit, Now and ever, and unto ages of ages.

Amen.

St Kevin and the Blackbird

The glen of Glendalough, even in the time of its ancient silence, was a deep, solitary cut in the emerald earth where water wept over stone and the air hung heavy with prayer.

Here lived Kevin, a saint who loved the world so much he sought to leave its clamor entirely, hoping to find God not in the marketplace, but in the unwavering hush of the eternal hills.

He lived in a tiny cell, woven of wicker and faith, a space barely large enough to kneel, and there he sought his Lord with constant, unmoving prayer. Kevin was known to hold his arms out wide like a cross, seeking to mirror the sacrifice of his Master, and in this posture of pure obedience, he often remained until the morning chill had thawed.

One bright, cold morning, as he knelt thus, his right arm stretched out, his palm held open toward the grey sky, a wonder occurred that would seal his legend forever. A Blackbird, feathered icon of song, mistook his warm, motionless palm for the sturdy branch of an ancient oak, and settled there without fear.

And that was only the start of the miracle.

The little blackbird began her work with the fierce, focused energy of a creature serving a divine purpose. Twig by twig, blade of moss by blade of moss, she wove her home upon the quiet hollow of the Saint's outstretched palm, finding in its unwavering stillness the perfect cradle. Kevin saw the delicate sanctuary forming, a vessel for new life. He knew that to move—to reclaim his body for even a moment—would be to shatter this fragile hope, spilling forth not egg or chick, but the very promise of God's smallest blessings.

Kevin, who understood the whispering wisdom of the wild, did not stir. He remained, a living, breathing, unwavering pillar of the living earth, his heart a chapel of calm. For days that turned into weeks, he held his sacred vigil. The sun warmed him by day, a gentle kiss upon his skin; the cool mists of the glen wrapped him in a soft, dewy embrace by night. Though his body grew weary, his spirit knew no strain. His soul sang a silent, ceaseless prayer of acceptance: 'Let this tiny creature find her rest in Thee, O Lord, and in my joyful willingness to serve the smallest of Thy children.' He became part of the very landscape, a holy bridge between the human and the feathered world, visible only to God and the passing deer, until the fledglings were strong enough to take their first, sweet flight, carrying their song of joy into the morning air.

He became part of the very landscape, a holy bridge between the human and the feathered world, visible only to God and the passing deer. When the eggs were laid, and then when the tiny, yellow beaks finally broke the shells, crying for life and nourishment, Kevin still held firm. He was a living branch of compassion, rooted in the love that suffers all things, until the fledglings were strong enough to take their first, sweet flight, carrying their song of joy into the morning air.

It is said that when the last bird flew, Kevin's arm, which had been a living branch for so long, felt a new lightness, a deeper strength than ever before—the strength that comes from perfect, humble sacrifice and boundless, shared joy.

God had witnessed his profound love, and the little blackbird had left behind a blessing woven of moss, grace, and the unforgettable melody of new life.

Psalm of the Wild: The Blackbird's Song
(for St Kevin and the Blackbird)

O Lord God, Fashioner of the visible and invisible, Who hast arrayed the fields in verdure and the firmament in song: At the breaking of dawn, the blackbird lifts its throat in psalmody,

A living icon of Thy mercy, woven in the rays of Thy unwaning Light. Glory to Thee, O Bestower of wings and spirit to all Thy works, Who dost breathe life into the dust and call forth praise from every tongue. In the hush of the glen, its melody resounds as ceaseless doxology, Bearing witness to Thy providence, boundless as the heavens. Instruct us, O Christ, to adore with contrite souls, That we may chant in symphony with beasts and birds, Thy handiwork redeemed.

As Thy holy one, Kevin, became a living sanctuary for the nest in outstretched palm, Vouchsafe us communion with all Thy creation, transfigured in Thy grace.

Glory to the Father, and to the Son, and to the Holy Spirit, Now and ever, and unto ages of ages.

Amen.

In the cold, bright heart of the Northumbrian coast, where the wind sang its ancient songs across the sea, lived Father Cuthbert. He was known throughout the land for his gentle spirit, but he longed for a silence deeper than any earthly shore could offer, where his soul could speak directly to God. At last, he settled on the lonely, craggy Farne Island, a place so remote that only the seabirds nested there, and where the waves struck the rock with the solemnity of a ceaseless prayer.

In this solitary sanctuary, Cuthbert sought to purify his spirit through constant prayer and unwavering devotion. Often, when the night drew deepest, the Saint would leave his cell and walk to the ocean's edge, entering the cool, cleansing waves. There, he would chant the psalms until the water covered his shoulders, allowing the vastness of the sea to envelop him in a powerful, unspoken communion with his Creator. It was a baptism of discipline, a way to chase all earthly burdens from his soul with the fire of heavenly love.

One night, a fisherman huddled near the coast saw a gentle glow emanating not from a ship, but from the very sea itself. He watched, astonished and filled with reverence, as the figure of Cuthbert emerged from the shimmering waves and knelt upon the dark shore to continue his prayer. A chill settled upon the Saint, for the night air was sharp, and his body was quiet with the stillness of deep contemplation.

Then, from the water, came two creatures of slick, dark fur—two otters, who were the gentle kin of the river and the sea. They did not flee from the praying man, but instead approached him with the trusting grace of old friends. With great tenderness, the little otters began to rub and lick the Saint's feet and his lower limbs, sharing their own vibrant warmth and their deep, natural kindness. When they were satisfied the quiet chill had lifted, they nestled their dark heads close to his knees for a moment, as if in silent blessing, and then slipped back into the waves, disappearing without a sound.

The fisherman rushed to the island the next morning, expecting to find the Saint weary from his vigil, but Cuthbert was in his cell, radiating an uncommon peace. He had felt the touch of the Divine through the humblest of creatures, a gentle sign that his solitary devotion was witnessed and profoundly blessed. The little otters had not been mere beasts of the dark waters, but messengers of grace, teaching that true faith is always rewarded with unexpected warmth and the deep companionship of all creation.

Psalm of the Wild: Waters of Healing
(For St. Cuthbert and the Otters)

O God of the living waters, Who dost purify and quicken the cosmos, Thou that renewest the face of the earth with Thy life-giving streams: Attend to the murmur of brooks and the gambol of otters in Thy providence, Thy humble servants mirroring the joy of Thy sanctifying flood.

Bless Thou the founts that sustain all mortal frames and verdant growth, That through font and flood, Thy healing virtue may flow unceasing. Bestow tranquility upon river and mere, upon abyss and wave, That every thirsting soul may quaff the draught of Thy divine mercy. Teach us, O Savior, to tread softly by these sacred courses, Honoring Thy wild kin as vessels of Thy hidden glory.

In their mirth, reveal Thy tender compassions anew, And in their frolic, a troparion of resurrectional praise.

Glory to the Father, and to the Son, and to the Holy Spirit, Now and ever, and unto ages of ages. Amen.

St Brendan and the Whale

The tale of Brendan the Voyager is not a story for maps and charts, but a testament to faith vast enough to navigate any sea. The Saint had gathered twelve brothers, and with hearts set firmly on God, they vowed to sail west into the Endless Ocean, seeking the fabled Land Promised to the Saints. They built a simple boat of hides stretched over a wooden frame, and with a prayer on their lips, cast themselves entirely upon the great, benevolent will of the water.

For many seasons they sailed, sustained by the ocean's bounty and sheltered beneath the vaulted, unblinking sky. Yet, as the great feast of Pascha—Easter—drew near, a gentle yearning settled upon them. It was a holy day, requiring a steadfast altar for the sacred service, but the wind-swept waves offered no steady ground, only endless motion.

One night, after much fervent prayer and hopeful expectation, Brendan spied a vast, low-lying expanse, flat and dark, seemingly unmoving in the twilight sea. It shimmered with a strange, pebbled surface. "Brothers," he said, his voice quiet with awe, "Behold, God has provided our Paschal table."

With joyful hearts, they disembarked and kindled a small fire on the strange, firm earth to cook their Paschal meal. They raised their voices in hymns, celebrating the Resurrection with deepest gratitude. But as the fire grew warm and the chanting grew fervent, the very island beneath them began to quiver and stir. The dark, flat land gave a slow, deep breath, and the pebbled surface began to shift, revealing great, ancient plates of barnacle-crusted skin.

It was no island at all, but a whale of leviathan size, the mightiest of the deep, who had found a quiet slumber near the surface. The gentle warmth of their small fire had roused it from its peaceful rest.

A momentary hush fell upon the monks, and then a ripple of awe, as the immense creature began its slow descent into the boundless waves. But as its colossal form disappeared beneath the shimmering surface, Brendan raised his hand not in alarm, but in solemn blessing. He called out to the great beast, his voice carrying over the waters: "Fear not, magnificent friend! You are one of God's grandest mysteries, and your patient rest has been a holy sanctuary for us. We offer our deepest thanks for your unwitting grace."

The whale, it is said, did not simply vanish. It gave a great, resonant exhale of water, a sound like a profound amen, which seemed to carry a message of deep, peaceful understanding and affirmation. It had offered its mighty body as an altar, not by human command, but by divine participation in the sacred feast.

For seven years thereafter, on every Pascha, the same benevolent whale, which Brendan named Jasconius, would rise in the very same spot to serve as the living, temporary land where the Saint and his brothers could celebrate their most sacred feast—a testament that even the unimaginable depths of the ocean are profoundly governed by heavenly mercy and sacred rhythm.

Psalm of the Wild: Ocean's Praise
(For St. Brendan and the Whale)

O Master of tempests and tranquil deeps, Ruler of abyssal realms and vaulted skies, Who dost still the raging surge and hallow the unplumbed mysteries: From the heart of the sea, the whale intones its resonant anthem, an oblation of sound ascending as sweet savor before Thy throne.

Impart boldness to Thy pilgrims upon the boundless waves, That in gale and calm alike, we may cleave to Thy unerring pilotage. As Brendan the voyager traversed the measureless ocean in faith, So conduct us, O Word, to the haven of Thy eternal kingdom. Let every creature intone the undying hymnody of Thy lovingkindness, From briny bed to empyrean height, in one voice of transfigured wonder.

For Thou hast knit all in the bond of Thy incarnate mercy, And through Thy cross, the waters of chaos are made wellsprings of life.

Glory to the Father, and to the Son, and to the Holy Spirit, Now and ever, and unto ages of ages. Amen.

St Hilda and the Swans

Hilda, the Abbess of Whitby, was a woman of noble blood and a spirit as pure as the white cliffs that cradled her monastery. She led a community of devoted souls with a wisdom that quietly influenced kings and a gentle patience that softened even the roughest hearts.

But her kindness was not kept only for humankind; her boundless compassion extended to every living thing that came within sight of her abbey on the headland.

The wind off the North Sea, a playful giant at times, could also turn blustery and wild, driving sudden squalls across the coast. And it was in one such blustery turn of weather that the gentle miracle of the swans unfolded.

A great flock of wild swans, majestic travelers of the air and water, were journeying south, high above the lively waves.

The gusting winds caught them in an unexpected tangle. Dazzled by the driving rain and weary from their long flight, many were buffeted. Some, disoriented, found themselves drawn too close to the jagged rocks below the cliff. Yet, many others, by some instinct deeper than their fear, managed to glide to a weary landing near the abbey grounds.

There they lay, their powerful wings drooping,
their feathers dampened by the sea mist,
their calls soft and plaintive.

When the bluster finally settled into a manageable sigh, Saint Hilda herself came down from the abbey with her novices. She carried baskets of woven straw and walked gently among the distressed flock. Hilda saw not mere birds, nor creatures ruined by the storm, but feathered pilgrims in need of succor, precious children of God's own design.

Hilda, with the practical wisdom that was her hallmark, directed her community to build small, sheltered pens where the swans could find safe refuge from the persistent wind and cold. She personally tended to the most weary, carefully supporting their drooping wings, cleaning their ruffled feathers, and offering them food by hand until their strength returned. Through the long, quiet weeks, the monastery bloomed into a sanctuary of silent, tender healing.

Not one bird, it is recorded, was lost under the Saint's watchful care. When their healing was complete, and the swans were fully recovered, they gathered on the green lawn outside the abbey walls. They lifted their mighty necks and gave a single, resonant chorus of unspoken praise—a magnificent, ethereal sound that carried across the waves and up to the heavens, a true hymn of gratitude. Then, with a flourish of perfect grace, they rose into the air, turning their strong wings toward the distant south.

They left behind a sense of profound peace and mutual reverence, having proven that the most powerful prayers are those offered not in grand words, but in the humble, life-giving act of nurturing all creation.

Psalm of the Wild: The Swan's Grace
(For St. Hilda and the Swans)

O Origin of comeliness and unassailable serenity, Whose wisdom directs the pinions of the airy host across the ether: We hymn Thee for the swan's silent majesty o'er the mirrored mere, A living symbol of purity, repose, and the radiance of Thy uncreated Light.

Upon the unruffled lake it glides with gentle power, Foreshadowing the renewal of souls in Thy baptismal stream. Bestow upon us spirits tranquil amid the tempests of this age, That we may yield to Thy governance with lowly trust.

As Thy handmaid Hilda shepherded the feathered throng with piety, So may we cherish Thy handiwork as icons of Thy sanctifying grace. Through her intercessions, enlighten our frailty with the purity of Thy saints, That in creation's chorus, we may behold Thy transfiguring face.

Glory to the Father, and to the Son, and to the Holy Spirit, Now and ever, and unto ages of ages. Amen.

St Tryphon and the Falcons

Now, if you journeyed far, far north in the old Russian lands, where the snow blankets the world for half the year and the forests hold secrets older than memory, you might hear tell of Saint Tryphon. He was no Tsar, nor a grand theologian with weighty tomes, but a man of such radiant simplicity, a holy fool, if you will, that his faith shone like a beacon. He lived his love for God with an unvarnished honesty that often made the worldly-wise scratch their heads, mistaking it for charming madness.

His greatest earthly delight, and his greatest earthly trial, was the building of a small, wooden monastery, dedicated to the Most Holy Trinity. It stood deep within the unbroken embrace of the taiga, and let me tell you, hauling logs and stones in the biting cold was no picnic! Yet, a peculiar difficulty arose, one born not of malice, but of plain, human need. The hungry folk from nearby settlements, seeing the monastery's modest stores, sometimes saw not a fortress of prayer, but their only slender hope for a winter meal.

Tryphon, whose heart knew no bounds when it came to compassion, found he simply could not refuse them. And so, the monastery's precious grain, intended for the baking of the Holy Bread—the very Body of Christ!—began to dwindle. But then, a second, rather more brazen challenge arrived, swooping from the sky itself: great flocks of bold, hungry birds, who descended upon the storehouses like a dark, feathered blessing for themselves, but a growing worry for the monks. Our poor brothers despaired, watching their winter survival vanish, morsel by precious morsel.

But Tryphon, their blessed Father, did not scold or fret. No, he simply walked out into the clearing, lifted his kind face to the vast, cold sky, and addressed the thieving flock. He spoke in the low, gentle tones one might use for an unexpected guest who had quite overstayed their welcome. He asked them, most politely, to leave. Not because he was a miser, mind you, but because this grain, this humble flour, was destined for the Sacrament, the bread that feeds not just the body, but the very soul. He promised, with absolute certainty, that if they would but respect this consecrated place, he himself would find them bounty in the abundant wild.

And then, children, the second marvel unfolded, a sight to quicken the heart! From the high, grey clouds, as if summoned by the very breath of God, came a squadron of swift, powerful Falcons, the true lords of the northern air. Now, these magnificent birds did not attack or harm the smaller, thieving visitors. No, they simply formed a silent, disciplined aerial guard, circling the monastery with tireless, sweeping wings. The presence of these fierce, unblinking sentinels was quite enough; the smaller birds, sensing the invisible boundary of a holy peace they dared not cross, fluttered away.

The Falcons remained for several days, keeping their perfect, noble vigil until all the precious stores were safely secured. When their sacred duty was done, they spiraled once, a magnificent, silent salute to the Saint, and disappeared back into the endless, azure sky. Tryphon smiled then, a deep, knowing smile, for he had seen the Divine Order made manifest: fierce strength employed not for the hunt, but for tender protection. A wondrous sign, indeed, that even the most powerful creatures are but willing servants of the simplest human prayer, offered from a heart brimful with love.

Psalm of the Wild: Wings of Protection
(For St. Tryphon and the Falcons)

O Guardian of the suppliant throng, Whose might upholds the frail and the fervent, In Thy puissance the falcon mounts the azure vault on tireless wing: With piercing gaze and silent grace, it guards the bounds of Thy holy peace, A celestial watchman o'er mountain and plain, Thy mighty hand unfurled. Have mercy, O Lord, and cover us beneath the overshadowing of Thy cherubic pinions, preserve us in the covert of Thy peace, amid all peril and strife.

As Thy confessor Tryphon stood blessed amidst the winged hosts in northern wilds, granted aid from the very sky, Direct us through every trial, fastening our souls in Thy invincible aid. Let every feathered herald proclaim Thy august Name on high, In exultant soar and ceaseless canticle, a liturgy of the winds.

For Thou hast arrayed Thy creatures in splendor, as harbingers of Thy kingdom, And in their heavenly vigil, we foretaste the dawn of the age to come.

Glory to the Father, and to the Son, and to the Holy Spirit, Now and ever, and unto ages of ages. Amen.

Archangel Michael and the Mountain Hawk

It is known throughout the whole of creation, from the shimmering choirs above to the quietest corners of the earth, that the Archangel Michael is the Grand Marshal of the heavenly host, the one who summons the incorporeal powers against all malice and encroaching darkness.

His presence is the scent of a wind made clean by divine fire, the blinding flash of a sword drawn for righteousness, and the absolute, unyielding certainty of divine justice. Yet, and here lies a truth profound as any ancient stone, the greatest protectors are often revealed not in the thunderous clamor of battle, but in the most subtle and quiet of signs.

The holy elders, those keepers of wisdom as old as the mountains themselves, speak of a time when a certain village, nestled high in the remote folds of the Caucasus, found itself steeped in a great and inexplicable spiritual malaise.

It was not famine, though the fields did indeed wither. It was not pestilence, though the children did inexplicably fall ill. No, it was a profound, suffocating gloom, a chill upon the spirit that settled over the place like a shroud woven of despair.

The villagers, with a stubborn faith forged in hardship, prayed and fasted with all their might, but the affliction clung to them, damp and pervasive, defying all earthly remedy.

They turned their tear-filled eyes heavenward,
begging for the swift intercession of Michael-

the Champion against

all
unseen
 foes.

The answer, when it came, was not in a sudden, dramatic vision that split the sky, nor in the clang of ethereal armor. No, it unfolded in the slow, unflinching daily vigil of a Mountain Hawk. This bird, majestic and tireless, a creature of stark precision and elemental grace, chose a single, towering crag overlooking the village as its permanent, sacred roost. From the first blush of dawn to the deep purple of dusk, it remained there, its gaze unblinking, surveying the entire valley with a silent, fierce intent. It neither pursued the quick, darting prey near the village nor soared away on errant currents to greener, distant slopes. It simply watched.

And so, the villagers, with their patient mountain wisdom, began to notice a curious thing: as the hawk held its silent, unwavering vigil, the oppressive feeling that had gripped their spirits slowly, imperceptibly, began to dissipate. It was as if the sheer, focused intensity of the creature's unblinking eye became a living shield against the creeping darkness, a bulwark woven of pure attention.

They understood the sign, a revelation as clear as a mountain spring: the great Archangel Michael, whose radiant form cannot be perceived by mortal eyes, had placed a living, breathing symbol of his own unslumbering watchfulness upon their very mountain.

The hawk became their Vigil of the Sky, a tangible promise etched against the azure. Its unmoving presence was a constant, profound reminder that the heavenly powers were indeed attending to their every need, not with the chaos of war, but with the steadfast order of divine love. They began to see in the hawk's perfect, unhurried circles a reflection of the vast, encompassing love of God, and in its sharp, unwavering sight, the merciless justice that would not suffer malice to thrive, yet offered protection to the innocent.

The villagers found their strength and courage renewed, not through the visible triumph of a sword or the blast of a trumpet, but through the humble, profound manifestation of perfect vigilance.

Eventually, as surely as winter yields to spring, the blight lifted, the fields flourished once more, and the children regained their laughter. And the hawk, its holy service completed, rose on the warm wind and flew away toward the sun-drenched peaks, leaving the valley not with a feeling of abandonment, but with the unshakeable knowledge of protection that had been granted to them, a grace as enduring as the mountains themselves.

Psalm of the Wild: The Hawk's Vigil
(For Archangel Michael and the Mountain Hawk)

O Archistrategos Michael, chief among the Incorporeal Powers, invincible champion against all darkness, Shield us with the living icon of the crag-dwelling hawk's unslumbering watch: Thy heavenly pinions cleave the firmament in all-encompassing sweep, an incorporeal ward o'er tor and dale, Thy flaming sword ever poised, ever victorious.

O Most Dread Commander, strengthen us in the fray of this shadowed sojourn, make us immovable in the bulwark of faith, ever radiant in undimmed expectation.

As Thine unwearying, all-seeing gaze surveys the heights unblinking, So attune our inward sight to the splendor of Thy sovereign love. With all Thy ministering spirits and the symphony of the visible world, We raise the angelic Trisagion, proclaiming Thy glory, O Lord, enthroned eternally.

For through Thee, O faithful warrior of the Most High, creation is upheld and guided towards its redemption, And the tempests of the adversary yield to the peace of the Age to Come.

Glory to the Father, and to the Son, and to the Holy Spirit, Now and ever, and unto ages of ages. Amen.

Age to Come
Pronunciation: /eɪdʒ tu: kʌm/
Definition or Context: The eschatological period following Christ's Second Coming, the resurrection of the dead, and the final judgment. It signifies the triumph over the adversary and the state of eternal blessedness, often referred to as the Eighth Day in Orthodox tradition, where creation is guided toward full redemption.
Source(s): Thematic/Eschatological Context.

Akolouthia (Ἀκολουθία)
Pronunciation: /æ.koʊˈlu:θi.ə/
Etymology: Greek, from akolouthein (to follow, accompany).
Definition or Context: In its liturgical sense, it refers to the order, sequence, or structure of an entire service (e.g., the Akolouthia of Vespers). In the context of the psalm, it is used poetically to mean an undying, endless procession or a continuous following of praise ascending to God.
Source(s): Liturgical Term; Eschatological Consummation (Final Psalm).

Amen (Ἀμήν)
Pronunciation: /aːˈmɛn/
Etymology: Hebrew, meaning "so be it," or "truly."
Definition or Context: A concluding word used at the end of prayers, hymns, and doxologies, signifying affirmation and agreement. In the narrative, it is described as the resonant exhale of the whale Jasconius, embodying a deep, peaceful understanding.
Source(s): Liturgical Usage; Thematic Narrative.

Anchorite (Ἀναχωρητής)
Pronunciation: /ˈæŋkəraɪt/
Etymology: Greek, from anakhorein (to withdraw, retreat).
Definition or Context: A Christian ascetic who withdraws from society to live a solitary life devoted to prayer, often living in a fixed, isolated location (unlike a wandering hermit). It is used metaphorically for the slow, crawling worm in the soil, referring to a solitary, spiritual entity.
Source(s): Monastic Term; Thematic/Poetic Language.

Antiphons **(Ἀντίφωνα)**
Pronunciation: /'æntɪfɒnz/
Etymology: Greek, from anti (in return) and phōnē (sound), meaning alternate sounding.
Definition or Context: Short verses or refrains sung or chanted alternately by two choirs or a priest and choir. The "avian antiphons" refer to the sweet, sharp calls of woodland choirs mentioned in the context of prayer, suggesting the natural world singing in alternating response to human prayer.
Source(s): Liturgical Term; Eschatological Consummation (Final Psalm).

Apolytikion (Ἀπολυτίκιον)
Pronunciation: /æpəluːˈtiːkiɒn/
Etymology: Greek, from apolyein (to dismiss).
Definition or Context: A dismissal hymn (a type of Troparion) sung near the end of Vespers and Orthros, and repeated during the Divine Liturgy. It summarizes the essence of the feast day or the life of the saint being commemorated.
Source(s): Liturgical Term; History of Non-Biblical Psalms (Hymnography).

Archangel Michael (Ἀρχάγγελος Μιχαήλ)
Pronunciation: /ɑːrkˈeɪndʒəl ˈmaɪkəl/
Etymology: From Greek archí (chief) and ángelos (messenger); Hebrew Mīkhā'ēl ("Who is like God?").
Definition or Context: The Grand Marshal of the heavenly host and one of the chief angelic figures. He is the champion against malice and darkness, often invoked for protection. He is given the title Archistratēgos (chief commander).
Source(s): Angelology; Thematic/Hagiographic Narrative.

Archistratēgos (Ἀρχιστράτηγος)
Pronunciation: /ɑːrkiːˈstrætɪgɒs/
Etymology: Greek, from archí (chief) and stratēgós (army leader).
Definition or Context: A title given exclusively to Archangel Michael, meaning chief commander or leader of the hosts (of the Heavenly Host).
Source(s): Angelology; Thematic/Hagiographic Narrative.

Askesis (Ἄσκησις)
Pronunciation: /'æs-kə-sɪs/
Etymology: Greek, meaning exercise, practice, or training.
Definition or Context: Spiritual discipline; the concerted effort a Christian makes toward perfection and communion with God. This includes fasting, vigil, prostrations, and prayer. In the author's context, the act of writing a psalm is considered a form of personal askesis and spiritual exertion.
Source(s): Monastic/Spiritual Term; Author's Justification.

Body of Christ
Pronunciation: /bɒdi ɒv kraɪst/
Definition or Context: Primarily refers to the consecrated Holy Bread (the Host or Lamb) used for the Sacrament of the Eucharist. The term also refers to the Church itself, the whole community of believers (Sobornost).
Source(s): Sacramental Term; Thematic Narrative.

Byzantine Hymnography
Pronunciation: /'bɪzən,taɪn hɪm'nɒɡrəfi/
Definition or Context: The dominant form of poetic composition in the Church developed during the Byzantine Empire (4th to 15th centuries). It is characterized by complex structures like the Kanon and served to articulate and popularize complex Christian doctrines.
Source(s): Liturgical History; History of Non-Biblical Psalms.

Canonical Catalogue
Pronunciation: /kə'nɒnɪkəl 'kætəlɒɡ/
Definition or Context: The formal, fixed, and official list of the Church's liturgical texts (like the Menaion, Triodion, etc.). The author humbly acknowledges that their work does not belong to this authoritative list.
Source(s): Liturgical Term; Author's Justification.

Canticle (Ὠιδή)
Pronunciation: /'kæntɪkəl/
Etymology: Latin canticulum (little song).
Definition or Context: Biblical odes (e.g., the Song of Moses, the Magnificat) used in the structure of the Kanon. Used thematically, it refers to a ceaseless song, such as the "liturgy of the winds."
Source(s): Liturgical Term; History of Non-Biblical Psalms (Hymnography); Thematic/Poetic Language.

Catechesis (Κατήχησις)
Pronunciation: /kætəˈkiːsɪs/
Etymology: Greek, from katēkheō (to instruct orally, resound).
Definition or Context: The act of religious instruction or teaching of the Christian faith and doctrine to new or existing believers. The book's overarching purpose is described as an effort in catechesis and piety.
Source(s): General Religious Term; Author's Justification.

Charism (Χάρισμα)
Pronunciation: /ˈkærɪzəm/
Etymology: Greek, meaning favor or gift.
Definition or Context: A supernaturally conferred gift or grace given by the Holy Spirit for the benefit of the Church. It is used in the narrative to describe the ability to decipher the language of untamed solitudes.
Source(s): Theological Term; Thematic Narrative.

Cherubic Pinions
Pronunciation: /tʃəˈruːbɪk ˈpɪnjənz/
Etymology: Cherubic from Hebrew kərūḇīm (plural of Cherub); Pinions from Latin penna (feather).
Definition or Context: The wings of the Cherubim, one of the highest orders of angels, known for their deep knowledge and constant worship of God. They are associated with God's presence and protection (e.g., the Ark of the Covenant).
Source(s): Angelology; Thematic/Liturgical Language.

Christological Doctrines
Pronunciation: /kraɪstəˈlɒdʒɪkəl ˈdɒktrɪnz/
Definition or Context: The body of teachings and theological principles concerning the person, nature, and role of Jesus Christ (e.g., that Christ is fully God and fully Man). Early hymns were crucial in articulating and defending these doctrines against heresies.
Source(s): Theological Term; History of Non-Biblical Psalms (Hymnography).

Cosmos (Κόσμος)
Pronunciation: /ˈkɒzmɒs/
Etymology: Greek, meaning order, good order, or a regulated world.
Definition or Context: Refers to the visible and invisible creation,

called forth by God in sophia (wisdom). It is often contrasted with chaos.
Source(s): Theological Term; Eschatological Consummation (Final Psalm).

Deified / Deifying Radiance (Θέωσις / Θεοτική ἀκτὶς)
Pronunciation: /'diːɪfaɪd / θeɪoʊ'tɪk 'reɪdɪəns/
Definition or Context: Related to Theosis (deification), the process of human beings becoming like God (or creation being transfigured in God's light) through grace. Deifying Radiance (theotic radiance) refers to the uncreated light of God that sanctifies creation, causing it to ascend the spiritual "ladder of divine union."
Source(s): Theological Term; Thematic/Theological Context; Eschatological Consummation.

Doxology (Δοξολογία)
Pronunciation: /dɒk'splədʒi/
Etymology: Greek, from doxa (glory) and logia (speaking).
Definition or Context: A liturgical expression of praise to God, typically the Holy Trinity. The standard phrasing is the Lesser Doxology ("Glory to the Father, and to the Son, and to the Holy Spirit, Now and ever, and unto ages of ages").
Source(s): Liturgical Term.

Economy (Οἰκονομία)
Pronunciation: /ɪ'kɒnəmi/
Etymology: Greek, from oîkos (house) and némein (to manage), meaning household management.
Definition or Context: God's vast, benevolent plan for creation and humanity's redemption. It refers to the order, administration, and purpose of all created things. Creatures are considered ensouled entities within God's boundless, singing Economy.
Source(s): Theological Term; Thematic/Theological Context; Eschatological Consummation.

Eschatological Consummation (Ἔσχατον / Συντέλεια)
Pronunciation: /ɛskətə'lɒdʒɪkəl kɒnsə'meɪʃən/
Etymology: Eschatological from Greek éskhatos (last); Consummation from Latin consummare (to complete).
Definition or Context: The title of the final psalm, referring to the end times and the completion or culmination of God's plan for creation, culminating in the Parousia (Second Coming).
Source(s): Title/Thematic Context.

Eucharistia (Εὐχαριστία)
Pronunciation: /juːkərɪˈstiːə/
Etymology: Greek, meaning thanksgiving.
Definition or Context: Primarily refers to the Sacrament of Holy Communion. Used in the author's context, it refers to gratitude, with the act of creating a psalm being an act of personal eucharistia and Eucharistic bond (fellowship of praise).
Source(s): Sacramental Term; Author's Justification; Eschatological Consummation (Final Psalm).

Folia (Private Piety)
Pronunciation: /ˈfoʊliə ˈpaɪəti/
Etymology: Latin folium (leaf, page), suggesting small, personal writings or prayers.
Definition or Context: The Tradition of Folia refers to the Church's encouragement of the creation of personal, non-liturgical prayers and devotional practices that flow from a believer's heart, supplementing the formal services.
Source(s): Theological Term; Author's Justification.

Heresies (Αἱρέσεις)
Pronunciation: /ˈhɛrɪsiz/
Etymology: Greek, from hairesis (choice, selection, a self-chosen opinion).
Definition or Context: Incorrect theological teachings that are contrary to the dogma of the Church and threaten the unity of the faithful. Early hymnography was critical in defending the faith against major heresies (like Arianism or Nestorianism).
Source(s): Theological Term; History of Non-Biblical Psalms (Hymnography).

Hymnography (Ὑμνογραφία)
Pronunciation: /hɪmˈnɒɡrəfi/
Etymology: Greek, from hýmnos (hymn) and graphía (writing).
Definition or Context: The vast body of original, non-Biblical poetic compositions developed by the Church to express theology, praise, and supplication. It is distinct from the 150 Biblical Psalms.
Source(s): Liturgical Term; History of Non-Biblical Psalms (Hymnography).

Icon (Εἰκών)
Pronunciation: /ˈaɪkɒn/
Etymology: Greek, meaning image or likeness.
Definition or Context: A visible, holy image used in Orthodox worship that points toward the prototype (Christ, the Mother of God, or the Saints). Theologically, every person is an icon of God. Creatures are referred to as "fellow icons of the Living God" or "breathing icons of the wild."
Source(s): Theological/Artistic Term; Thematic/Theological Context.

Kanon (Κανών)
Pronunciation: /ˈkænɒn/
Etymology: Greek, meaning rule, measuring stick, or standard.
Definition or Context: The dominant form of Byzantine hymnography, a complex poetic composition structured around nine Canticles (Biblical odes). It is sung at the service of Orthros (Matins). St. John of Damascus is a chief master of the Kanon.
Source(s): Liturgical Term; History of Non-Biblical Psalms (Hymnography).

Kenosis (Κένωσις)
Pronunciation: /kəˈnoʊsɪs/
Etymology: Greek, meaning self-emptying or making oneself void.
Definition or Context: The theological concept describing Christ's voluntary self-limitation by taking on human form (Philippians 2:7). It is the model for Christian humility. In the psalm, the Saints walk with creation in trusting kenosis, emphasizing their humility and self-denial.
Source(s): Theological Term; Eschatological Consummation (Final Psalm).

Kontakion (Κοντάκιον)
Pronunciation: /kɒnˈtækiɒn/
Etymology: Greek, possibly referring to the pole (kontos) around which the scroll was wrapped.
Definition or Context: An older form of Byzantine hymnography, consisting of a long, verse-upon-verse homily set to music, popular up until the 7th century. It is now usually reduced to a short hymn sung at the Divine Liturgy.
Source(s): Liturgical Term; History of Non-Biblical Psalms (Hymnography).

Nous (Νοῦς)
Pronunciation: /nuːs/ or /naʊs/
Etymology: Greek, meaning mind, intellect, or spiritual perception.
Definition or Context: In Orthodox theology, it is the highest faculty of the soul, the "eye of the heart" that is capable of direct, intuitive knowledge of God. The prayer asks for the human nous to be "knit to the panoply of breathing forms" in a spiritual bond.
Source(s): Theological/Philosophical Term; Eschatological Consummation (Final Psalm).

Pantocrator (Παντοκράτωρ)
Pronunciation: /pænˈtɒkrətɔːr/
Etymology: Greek, from pas (all) and kratos (strength, power), meaning Ruler of All or Almighty.
Definition or Context: A major title for God the Father or Christ, especially common in Byzantine iconography, where Christ is depicted as the majestic and compassionate Lord of the Universe.
Source(s): Theological/Artistic Term; Eschatological Consummation (Final Psalm).

Parousia (Παρουσία)
Pronunciation: /pəˈruːsiːə/
Etymology: Greek, meaning presence or arrival.
Definition or Context: The theological term for the Second Coming of Christ and the final manifestation of God's Kingdom. The final psalm asks for God's Name to be hymned in the parousia of all things renewed.
Source(s): Eschatological Term; Eschatological Consummation (Final Psalm).

Piety (Εὐσέβεια)
Pronunciation: /ˈpaɪəti/
Etymology: Latin pietas (dutiful conduct).
Definition or Context: Religious devotion and reverence; the practical application of faith in daily life. The book is presented as an effort in catechesis and piety.
Source(s): General Religious Term; Thematic Context.

Platytera (Πλατυτέρα)
Pronunciation: /plætɪˈtɛrə/
Etymology: Greek, a shortened form of Platytera ton Ouranon ("Wider than the Heavens").
Definition or Context: An iconic title for the Mother of God (Theotokos), depicting her with Christ in her womb/breast, symbolizing that she contains the Uncontainable God and is thus "Wider than the Heavens." The whale is metaphorically called a platytera of the sea, emphasizing its vastness as a living cathedral.
Source(s): Theological/Iconographic Term; Thematic/Poetic Language.

Sobornost (Соборность)
Pronunciation: /səˈbɔːrnəst/
Etymology: Russian, from sobor (council, cathedral, or assembly).
Definition or Context: A theological and philosophical term, distinct to Russian Orthodoxy, emphasizing the organic unity, conciliarity, and communal spirit of the Church. It is the unity of many freely united individuals, which the final psalm celebrates as the unity of Creation in Christ.
Source(s): Orthodox/Theological Term; Eschatological Consummation (Final Psalm Subtitle).

Theophany (Θεοφάνεια)
Pronunciation: /θiːˈɒfəni/
Etymology: Greek, from theós (God) and phainein (to appear).
Definition or Context: A visible manifestation of God's invisible glory or presence to humanity. The Fathers taught that all creation is a theophany—a continuous showing forth of God's power and beauty.
Source(s): Theological Term; Thematic/Theological Context.

Theosis (Θέωσις)
Pronunciation: /θiːˈoʊsɪs/
Etymology: Greek, meaning deification.
Definition or Context: The Orthodox theological doctrine that humanity's goal is to become like God or partakers of the divine nature (2 Peter 1:4) through Christ's grace. The holy ones achieved Theosis in their interaction with the wild kin, signifying a return to the pre-Fall relationship.
Source(s): Theological Term; Thematic/Theological Context.

Troparion (Τροπάριον)
Pronunciation: /troʊˈpɑːrɪɒn/
Etymology: Greek, possibly from tropos (turn, mode).
Definition or Context: A short, pithy stanza or hymn summarizing a feast or saint's life, or expressing a theological theme. The Apolytikion is a specific type of Troparion. The "age-abiding Troparion" refers to the core hymn of praise that creation continually sings.
Source(s): Liturgical Term; History of Non-Biblical Psalms (Hymnography); Eschatological Consummation.

Transfiguring Face
Pronunciation: /trænsˈfɪgjərɪŋ feɪs/
Definition or Context: A direct theological reference to the Transfiguration of Christ on Mount Tabor, where His glory was revealed in uncreated light. It symbolizes the glorified, radiant appearance of Christ that believers hope to behold. The prayer asks to see this Face reflected in creation's chorus.
Source(s): Theological Term; Thematic/Theological Language.

Trinitarian Doctrines
Pronunciation: /trɪnɪˈtɛəriən ˈdɒktrɪnz/
Etymology: Latin trinitas (the number three).
Definition or Context: The body of teachings concerning the nature of the Holy Trinity—God as one essence (ousia) in three hypostases (Father, Son, and Holy Spirit). Early hymns were essential in articulating and defending these doctrines (like that of the Filioque debate, which is rejected by Orthodoxy).
Source(s): Theological Term; History of Non-Biblical Psalms (Hymnography).

Trisagion (Τρισάγιον)
Pronunciation: /traɪˈsægiɒn/
Etymology: Greek, from tris (thrice) and hagios (holy), meaning Thrice-Holy.
Definition or Context: The ancient liturgical hymn: "Holy God, Holy Mighty, Holy Immortal, have mercy on us." It is sung multiple times during the Divine Liturgy and other services. It is often referred to as the song of the angelic hosts.
Source(s): Liturgical Term; Thematic/Liturgical Language.

Vespers (Ἑσπερινός)
Pronunciation: /ˈvɛspərz/
Etymology: Latin vesper (evening).
Definition or Context: The major daily service traditionally celebrated in the late afternoon or early evening. It serves as the beginning of the new liturgical day (since the Church day begins at sunset). Idiomelon/Stichera verses are interspersed during this service.
Source(s): Liturgical Term; History of Non-Biblical Psalms (Hymnography).

Vouchsafe
Pronunciation: /vaʊtʃˈseɪf/
Etymology: Middle English, from vouch (to guarantee) and safe (safe, sure).
Definition or Context: An older English term meaning to grant or give in a gracious or condescending manner. In a prayer, it is a humble request for God to grant a great spiritual gift (e.g., requesting the charism of the primordial chant).
Source(s): Poetic/Liturgical Language; Thematic/Poetic Language.

Word Incarnate
Pronunciation: /wɜːrd ɪnˈkɑːrnət/
Etymology: Latin in (in) and caro (flesh).
Definition or Context: A title for Jesus Christ, referring to the second person of the Holy Trinity (the Logos or Word) having taken on human flesh. This is the central tenet of the Incarnation.
Source(s): Theological Term; Thematic/Theological Context.

The Icon and the Idol—A Contested Terrain of Compassion

The psalms preceding this threshold have sounded a liturgy drawn from the very sinews of creation. Hopefully, they resonate with a more profound and ancient, sanctified truth: that the terrestrial sphere is a vibrant **theophany**, a ceaseless manifestation of God's uncreated energies. Within the Orthodox Christian tradition, as these hymns attest, the animal kingdom is viewed not merely as a resource or a collection of biological entities, but as an integral, participating element in the cosmic drama of salvation and deification.

This vision hinges on two core theological principles: **The Animal as Icon** and the potential for **Theosis in the Ktisis** (Creation).

The Orthodox veneration of the Icon is the key. An icon is not an idol to be worshipped, but a 'window into heaven' that points beyond itself to the Prototype. Animals, by their very existence, and especially in their purity and untamed fidelity to their created Logos (the divine blueprint), serve as living icons. They reflect the unblemished glory of the Creator. Their innocence is a standing reproach to fallen humanity, and in the lives of the saints—St. Kevin, St. Cuthbert, St. Brendan, St. Tryphon—the wild creatures become communion partners, co-liturgists, and heralds of the eschatological peace. This is the Theopoia (divine making or poetry) of creation; the saint's transfigured, Christ-like nature restores the primordial relationship, allowing the 'Beast to Speak Blessing' once more. The ultimate trajectory is not merely welfare, but the Transfiguration of the cosmos, where all of creation, redeemed by the Incarnation, will ascend the ladder of divine union.

The Contested Cosmos (An Exposition of the Theme)

The liturgy just sounded has resonated with an ancient, sanctified truth: that the terrestrial sphere is a vibrant **theophany**, a ceaseless manifestation of God's uncreated energies. For the Orthodox Christian, the animal kingdom is an integral element in the cosmic drama of salvation and deification. This vision centers on the principle of the Animal as Icon—a living window into the Creator's glory—and **the potential for Theosis in the Ktisis (Creation)**.

The Problem of the Groaning Creation: Addressing Terror and Predation

We must immediately acknowledge the formidable counter-evidence: The animal world is not a peaceful kingdom. It is a realm of profound violence. Animals kill and devour each other relentlessly; humanity subsists by taking animal life; and creatures, from great predators to microscopic parasites, actively harm and kill human beings. Furthermore, human history is defined by men killing men, often driven by depravity and the enjoyment of suffering.

How can such a violent, anarchic system be reconciled with the proposition that the world is a window to divine peace? It cannot, if we fail to recognize the theological impact of the Fall.

The Orthodox view does not deny the brutality; it explains it. Predation is not the original Logos of creation; it is a symptom of the cosmic illness initiated by Adam's sin. As the Apostle Paul writes, *"The creation itself also will be delivered from the bondage of corruption into the glorious liberty of the children of God. For we know that the whole creation groans and labors with birth pangs together until now"* (Romans 8:21-22).

The harmony the saints achieve—the otters warming St. Cuthbert's feet, the blackbird nesting in St. Kevin's palm—are not quaint fables. They are flashes of the eschatological peace; temporary restorations of the unfallen dialogue, achieved through the *theosis* of the saint. They are prophecies made real, demonstrating that while the creation groans, it is also groaning toward redemption in Christ.

From Theology to Praxis: The Orthodox Ethic of Consumption

This rigorous framework informs the Orthodox ethic of stewardship, which contrasts sharply with both industrial exploitation and secular abolitionism. The Orthodox tradition does not call for the cessation of human use of animals, but for its sanctification and reorientation toward reverent stewardship and eucharistic use.

Farming and Hunting: If the animal is a living Icon, its use for food demands dignity and profound respect, not exploitation. The

Orthodox "way to farm" would prioritize the animal's natural well-being and logos even as it is raised for sustenance. The taking of life—whether in the field or the hunt—must be done quickly and with minimal suffering, rooted not in cold efficiency but in reverence for the life surrendered. Every meal becomes an act necessitating a prayer of gratitude and penitence, acknowledging that our nourishment requires the surrender of a fellow creature's life due to the post-lapsarian condition.

The Russian Bear: This vision finds cultural expression in anecdotes, particularly from the Orthodox Slavic world, of a more primal, familial interaction with the wild. Stories of saints like St. Seraphim of Sarov feeding bread to a bear, or contemporary tales of Russians interacting with the great predator, testify to a profound cultural memory. These are not merely foolish risks, nor are they a naive idealization of the wild (as illustrated tragically by Werner Herzog's *Grizzly Man*). They are cultural artifacts of the **Eschaton**, reminding us that the possibility of peace remains, and that the saint, through Christ, can restore the shattered boundary between human and animal.

The Immanent Haze: Responding to Cosmic Indifference
Yet, we must confront the final, most profound challenge—the voice of cosmic nihilism: "Nothing human has ever mattered to this world. Nothing human has ever excited the interest of rivers or flowers. Everything fades away in the specks of this blurred haze that the fire of the sun has added to the heat of the light every morning."

This sentiment perfectly articulates the worldview that strips nature of all transcendence, leaving it a silent, mechanical process utterly unconcerned with human destiny. It denies the possibility of the **Theophany and the Icon**.

The Orthodox response to this crushing indifference is rooted in one, singular, unassailable Event: **The Incarnation of the Logos.**

God did not become an indifferent spirit; He became Man. He entered the *oikonomia* (economy) of creation at the human level, thereby eternally investing human nature—and through human nature, the entire material world—with unimaginable significance. The river does not ignore humanity; it is rather humanity, in its fallen state, that struggles to hear the river's hymn. The blurring haze is not the final reality, but the shadow of corruption over the uncreated Light that illuminates all things.

Animals, God and Society

It is against this Christ-centered, eschatological view that we must contrast the radical secular philosophies of the animal rights movement, exemplified by organizations like People for the Ethical Treatment of Animals (PETA).

While both claim compassion, the Orthodox view is rooted in **Incarnational Theology** (God saving the flesh), whereas the PETA-style activist view is rooted in Utilitarian Philosophy (calculating suffering). The divergence is critical, for it necessitates confronting the hidden agendas of radical activism:

Deconstruction of *Imago Dei*: PETA's aggressive advocacy of speciesism—equating the moral distinction between a human and an animal with racism—is a direct assault on the biblical doctrine of humanity created in the Image of God. This seeks to dismantle the unique dignity conferred by the Incarnation.

The Abolitionist Endgame: The true goal is not better welfare but total Abolition: the termination of all human use of animals, including the ownership of pets, which is framed as "slavery." This agenda demands a revolutionary societal upheaval hostile to traditional human life and stewardship.

Controversial Means to Nihilistic Ends: The sensationalist campaigns and high-profile stunts employed by PETA are often strategic tools to deconstruct societal norms. Furthermore, the organization has faced intense criticism for its practices, including a high rate of euthanasia at its affiliated shelter facilities—a policy often defended as a necessary step toward preventing animals from being born into a world where humans might 'use' them. This tragic philosophy substitutes death for the potential for human care, fundamentally undermining the notion of loving custody.

This book, **When the Beasts Spoke Blessing: Threshold to a Hagiographic Odyssey**, is an invitation to reclaim a truly sacred and integrated understanding of the animal kingdom. It is a call to discern the difference between authentic, Christ-centered compassion and a secular, utilitarian movement that sees the animal as a tool for deconstructing human exceptionalism.

Let us cross this *limen* with contrite spirits, ready to hearken once more to the primordial dialogue of benediction.

In the shadowed vastness of a Moscow winter, where the snow falls like the tears of seraphim upon the onion domes of the Kremlin, one might stumble upon the heart of Russian Orthodoxy—not in some gilded theorem of the schools, but in the humble prostration of a *muzhik* before an icon that has gazed upon tsars and peasants alike. Ah, but what is this faith, this ancient fire kindled in the frozen north? It is no mere creed, scribbled in the dust of debate like the squabbles of English parsons over tea; it is a living paradox, a thunderclap of divine folly where God becomes man that man might become god—not in hubris, but in the quiet miracle of *theosis*, that slow transfiguration of the soul into the likeness of the Uncreated Light.

Picture it: the Trinity, Father, Son, and Spirit, not three gods in a quarrelsome committee, but one essence in eternal dance, a mystery so profound it mocks the measuring sticks of Western logic, yet so simple a child in the Volga mud might grasp it with a fistful of bread and a prayer.

Now, doctrine? Straight as a Cossack's saber, yet curving like the Neva in spring flood. The Incarnation: Christ, the Word made flesh, not some ethereal ghost haunting the margins of history, but a babe in the hay who sweats blood in Gethsemane and shatters death with a linen shroud. Sin is no abstract ledger of black marks; it is the rupture of communion, the soul's exile from the banquet hall of paradise. And salvation? Not a ticket punched at the gate, but a wedding feast where the guest is robed in grace, partaking of the very Body and Blood in the Eucharist—that central *mysteria*, the sacrament of sacraments, where bread and wine become, in ways past the probing of microscopes, the life of the world.

The other six follow suit: Baptism as drowning the old Adam in Jordan's chill; Chrismation, sealing the brows with holy oil like knights dubbed for battle; Confession, that raw American-style reckoning where you spill your guts to a black-robed father and rise unburdened; Holy Unction for the body's aches, a balm against the grave's shadow; Marriage, crowning love with thorns of endurance; Ordination, hands laid on to channel the apostolic fire. Each a door swung wide to the divine, no more negotiable than the Volga's inexorable flow.

But doctrine without practice is a lantern without oil—pretty, but pitch-black. In the Russian way, faith is no Sunday stroll in Hyde Park, bandying paradoxes with Chesterton's merry ghosts; it is the daily grind of the prayer rope, beads clicking like Hemingway's terse sentences through the Jesus Prayer: *"Lord Jesus Christ, Son of God, have mercy on me, a sinner."* Fifty times, a hundred—till the words sink into the bones like vodka into the blood, turning contemplation into communion.

Icons? Not idols, mind you, but windows cracked open to the eternal—Madonna and Child staring back from gold-leafed panels, saints in stiff brocade who intercede with the directness of a Lardner yarn, no frills, just *"Pray for us, you ragged lot of heaven's veterans."*

The Divine Liturgy? Ah, that's the crown: two hours of incense-thick air, chants rising like smoke from Siberian *taiga* fires, the priest's booming **"Peace be unto all!"** met with the people's thunderous **"And with thy spirit!"** It's communal, this worship— no lone ranger pew-sitting, but a throng swaying as one, crossing themselves right-to-left like sealing a vow against the devil's left-handed tricks.

And fasting? Forty days of Lent stripping the table to potatoes and prayer, a discipline sharp as a Siberian wind, teaching the belly who's master—not gluttony, but grace. Yet here's the Chestertonian twist in the Russian tale: amid tsarist chains and Bolshevik hammers, this Orthodoxy thrives on suffering's soil, *kenosis* writ large—the emptying of self that mirrors Christ's own. It's mystical, yes, veined with the *hesychast* silence of desert fathers transplanted to northern forests, where the soul stills to hear the uncreated light hum like a hidden river.

No puritan scowl here, but a joy paradoxical as Dickens' Micawber awaiting his next crumb of fortune: the Church as the ark of grace, unity in the Spirit's bond, a family sprawling from patriarch's throne to peasant's *izba*, where administration bends to mercy, not marble bureaucracy.

And in the end, straight talk like Hemingway sighting trout in the stream: this is no hobby for the half-hearted.

Dive in, cross yourself, taste the chalice—or stand forever on the riverbank, wondering at the splash.

The Russian Orthodox life? It's the whole blessed feast, served hot from heaven's kitchen, and you're invited, sinner though you be.

www.ingramcontent.com/pod-product-compliance
Lightning Source LLC
Chambersburg PA
CBHW071542120626
46550CB00006B/2556